# The Wolf

Story by
**ANITA TOWNSEND**

Pictures by
**MICHAEL ATKINSON**

*Exeter Books*

NEW YORK

Through the frozen pine forest, the she-wolf heard the call of her mate, and ran to join him. She pointed her muzzle to the sky and howled with him. She loved howling.

From far away, the other wolves of the pack came running in answer. Their eyes shone and they panted for breath in the cold air.

The wolves whined and waved their tails. And as each one came up with the leader it joined in the chorus of howling.

There were eight wolves in the pack: the she-wolf and her mate, five younger wolves and one old female, who was the weakest of them all.

Once all the wolves in the pack had arrived, they stopped howling. They waved their tails and sniffed and licked at each other in greeting. Then the leader of the pack trotted away, his tail held high. The she-wolf followed close behind, and the rest of the pack loped after them in single file. They were all very hungry for they had not made a kill for five days.

The wolves followed an old trail along a
ridge. After some time they caught the scent of
caribou. The pack stopped and gathered together,
nose to nose, waving their tails. Then they set off
to follow the scent. Before long, they spotted the
herd of caribou below them. The pack fanned out
in a half circle and crept slowly and quietly toward
their prey.

Suddenly the caribou noticed the wolves and turned to face them. There was a moment of silence. The wolves lay still, their yellow eyes fixed on their prey. Then one of the caribou turned and ran. As it dashed away, the rest of the herd panicked and ran too.

The wolves leaped after the running herd. As they ran, the she-wolf saw one of the younger caribou lagging behind the rest because it was lame. This was the one!

Quickly the wolves separated the young animal from its mother and closed in on it. The she-wolf leaped forward and snapped her teeth on the victim's rump. But the terrified creature shook her off and limped on.

Then, slowly bleeding from its wound, the caribou stopped and turned to face the wolves. The wolves stopped, too, and sank to the ground watching it. Their ears and the tips of their tails twitched slightly, and their eyes glinted. The wounded caribou had no chance. It could not fight. So it turned again and tried to run.

Instantly the wolves rushed forward. The she-wolf tore at its flanks. Her mate leaped for its throat. In a second, the calf was down, and the wolves were all over it. Blood stained the snow red.

Only the old wolf had been unable to keep up with the chase. Now she came up to the kill, tail between her legs. The other wolves would not let her eat until they had all gorged themselves. The she-wolf and her mate ate the best bits and the younger wolves seized limbs and bones and chewed at them, growling over their meal.

At last the bones were left for the old wolf to pick over. A flock of ravens that had been following the pack flapped down to join the feast. The other wolves rested in the shelter of a clump of pines on a ridge nearby. They all felt fat and full and sleepy.

When the pack moved off again, the old wolf stayed with the remains of the kill. She no longer had the strength to travel with the pack, who were ready to trek northward. Her teeth were blunt, her mate was dead. Without the pack she could only catch small animals, such as arctic hares or lemmings. She would become a lone wolf now, and roam the forest edges until she died.

It was the time of year when the females were ready to mate. One of the young females crept toward the leader of the pack. She whined and licked her lips and waved her tail at him. But the male wolf would not look at her, and his mate was furious. She rushed at the rival and drove her away, snarling and showing her sharp white teeth. The young female ran off, whimpering, her tail between her legs. She wanted to mate but the she-wolf would not let her. None but she would bear cubs in that pack, and she, herself, was ready to mate.

Then the pack leader came up to his mate, and sniffed at her. They licked each other and waved their tails. He danced around her, nipped at her face and ears and took her snout gently in his mouth. She nuzzled his fur and pushed her nose against his face. He bit gently at her neck and they mated.

Then they lay down together. The she-wolf made little fond grunts and whines to her mate. They had been mates for three years and would stay together. The other wolves crowded around the mating pair, but they did not disturb them.

When spring came, the pack was far in the north. The she-wolf looked for a place to make her den. She found an old burrow that had belonged to an arctic fox. It was near the top of a low sandy ridge, above a lake. This was a good place because the she-wolf could no longer travel far for water. Her cubs would soon be born. The pack leader helped the she-wolf clean the burrow and make it bigger. Deep inside they dug a smooth chamber ready for the cubs.

Every day the male put his scent on landmarks all around the den, and scratched up the earth round them. Any strange wolf that passed would smell the strong scent and keep away.

Three weeks later, the first cub was born. The she-wolf cleaned it, and licked it dry. Then she pushed the baby to her side with her nose, and curled around it. Safe and warm, they both rested in the darkness of the den.

The cub was covered in soft dark fur. Its eyes were closed and it squeaked faintly, but it could neither see nor hear. By morning five more cubs had been born. They staggered blindly around the den, watched by the pack leader who had come to see them. He licked them all over while his mate watched. Then she curled round them while they sucked milk from her.

As the cubs grew, all the pack brought food back for the mother, and helped to guard the family. The young female who had not mated often cleaned them or watched over them if their mother went away for a while. She would not let any male wolves except the father into the den.

Once, a grizzly bear smelled the baby wolves. He scratched and pawed at the entrance to the den. The mother wolf inside growled and snarled at him. Outside, the other wolves barked and worried at the bear. They nipped its heels and flanks, then darted away. Soon, the bear gave up and lumbered off. He would find some baby birds to eat instead of wolf cubs!

After three weeks the cubs came out of the den for the first time. Then every day they played in the sunshine outside. Soon, whenever any adult wolf came near, they would run over to it and lick its snout and cry and muzzle at its mouth. The wolf would then open its mouth and let them eat any half-digested food it had eaten. As well as this, they still liked to drink their mother's milk.

Besides playing, the little cubs fought each other, to prove which was the strongest.

One wolf cub, a gray one like his father, grew faster than the others, and was soon leader of the cubs. Once his mother had to pounce on him to stop him from harming one of his brothers. The she-wolf took the cub in her teeth and shook him. He whined and rolled over on his back. When his mother saw the pale fur on his belly she knew he had learned his lesson, and licked him instead of shaking him. None of the adult wolves liked to see the cubs fighting.

As the cubs grew older, their mother started to teach them to hunt. She brought them pieces of raw meat to chew and they learned to pounce on mice and lemmings in the grass.

By the time the cubs were six months old they were strong enough to run after the pack on short hunting trips. One day, the cubs were with the pack when they came across a herd of musk oxen. When the musk oxen saw the wolves, they formed a ring, with the bulls facing outward, protecting the cows and little calves in the center of their circle. The wolves howled but they did not dare attack the horned bulls. They slunk away to look for easier prey.

As the winter wore on, the wolf pack moved farther and farther south in search of caribou. By now, the cubs had shed their dark woolly fur and had grown thick coats of winter fur like the adults. They had learned how to catch arctic hares and grouse and how to howl. They ran with the pack, following their mother and her mate across the wastes of frozen snow.

# Wolf Facts

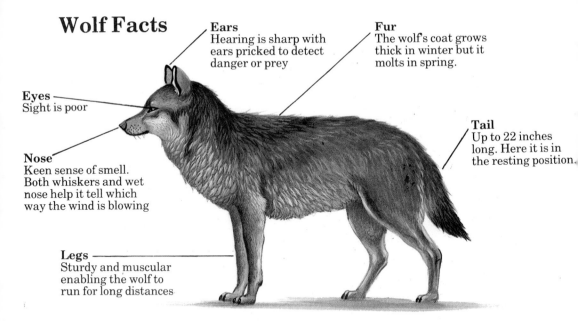

**Ears**
Hearing is sharp with ears pricked to detect danger or prey

**Fur**
The wolf's coat grows thick in winter but it molts in spring.

**Eyes**
Sight is poor

**Nose**
Keen sense of smell. Both whiskers and wet nose help it tell which way the wind is blowing

**Tail**
Up to 22 inches long. Here it is in the resting position.

**Legs**
Sturdy and muscular enabling the wolf to run for long distances

**The body of the gray wolf is between 3 and 5 feet long including the head**

Like people, no two wolves look exactly the same; each one is a slightly different color and size. There are two main types of wolf. The gray wolf in the story is the more common. The other kind, the red wolf, is not as large and it has a reddish coat. It lives only in a small area of North America. The gray wolf lives almost all over the northern half of the world.

## Hunters and Hunted
Once there were many many wolves, but there are fewer now because, for centuries, man has hunted the wolf wherever he has settled. Farmers believe that wolves are a threat to their sheep and cattle. But despite this, the wolves have managed to survive because they are such good hunters.

## What Wolves Eat
Wolves can live almost anywhere because they can eat so many kinds of food. Their favorite prey are big plant-eating animals such as moose or deer. But they will also eat smaller creatures such as sheep, hares, mice, birds and reptiles; and if they cannot get meat, they will eat fruit and berries.

## Tireless Travelers
When they eat, wolves eat a lot so that they can go for a long time without food. Wolves do not run very fast, except when running down a fleeing victim, but they can run for hours and hours without tiring. Sometimes the tracks and trails they use can be followed for more than 40 miles through mountains, forests and rivers.

## Working Together

The wolf is the ancestor of the dog, but the dog is no match for the wolf as a hunter. Wolves usually live and hunt in packs of between about ten and fifteen animals. By tracking and surrounding their prey together they can kill an animal large enough for a feast. All the members of the pack gain from this, especially the weaker ones. Lone wolves must live on the small animals they can catch on their own. They are also likely to be attacked by bigger animals who would never dare tackle a whole pack.

## Law and Order

Wolves can work as a group because they obey special rules. Each group has a leader whom the other wolves always obey. The leader always eats and drinks before the others and takes the best food for himself.

Each wolf under the leader has a special rank depending on its strength and skill. Wolves of a lower rank must obey and give place to wolves of a higher rank. This strict order prevents fighting. How they display their obedience is shown in the pictures on the right.

## Challenge for Leadership

Fights do sometimes occur; as a wolf grows stronger it may challenge a wolf of higher rank, even the leader. If it wins the fight, their positions are reversed and the loser must obey the new master. The loser lies on its back or crouches to show that it will not rebel. These rules ensure that the pack is led by the strongest, cleverest wolves.

### Who's Boss?

When two wolves meet, the higher ranking animal fluffs up its fur, pricks its ears and puts its tail in the air. The lower ranking wolf tries to look small, flattening its ears, crouching slightly and putting its tail between its legs. This shows that it will obey the stronger wolf. As long as it stays in this position, the stronger wolf will not hurt it. You can often see dogs behaving in the same way.

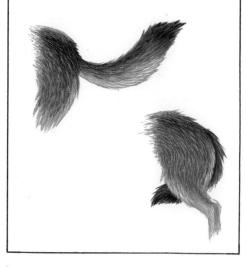

# More books for you to read from
## EXETER BOOKS

## WILDLIFE LIBRARY

If you have enjoyed this book, you will
be pleased to know that it is part of a
series:

> The Bear
> The Elephant
> The Deer
> The Wolf

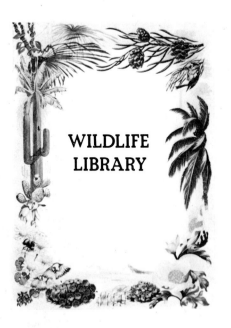

WILDLIFE
LIBRARY

## MY FIRST BOOK OF NATURE

In addition, there are six titles in
My First Book of Nature, a companion
series about the smaller creatures of
the countryside:

> The Duck
> The Butterfly
> The Squirrel
> The Fox
> The Frog
> The Mouse

All the books are in full color.

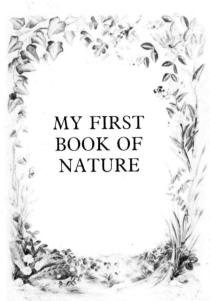

MY FIRST
BOOK OF
NATURE